Witness to History

The War
in Iraq

David Downing

www.heinemann.co.uk/library

Visit our website to find out more information about **Heinemann Library** books.

To order:

 Phone 44 (0) 1865 888066

Send a fax to 44 (0) 1865 314091

Visit the Heinemann Bookshop at www.heinemann.co.uk/library to browse our catalogue and order online.

First published in Great Britain by Heinemann Library,
Halley Court, Jordan Hill, Oxford
OX2 8EJ, part of Harcourt Education.
Heinemann is a registered trademark of
Harcourt Education Ltd.

Produced for Heinemann by Discovery Books Ltd
Editorial: Nancy Dickmann, Tanvi Rai and
 Kathryn Walker
Design: Rob Norridge and Ron Kamen
Picture Research: Rachel Tisdale
Production: Séverine Ribierre

Originated by Dot Gradations
Printed and bound in China by South China
Printing Company

ISBN 0 431 17074 6
08 07 06 05 04

British Library Cataloguing in Publication Data
Downing, David, 1946–
 The war in Iraq. – (Witness to History)
 956.7'0443

A full catalogue record for this book is available from
the British Library.

Acknowledgements
The publishers would like to thank the following for
permission to reproduce photographs: Corbis pp. 16
(Chris Collins), 22 (Pierre Schwartz), 23 (Lorenzo
Ciniglio), 26, 31 & 49 (Benjamin Lowy), 32 (Thorne
Anderson), 45 (Ed Kashi), 7, 47 & 48 (Lynsey Addario);
Corbis/Brooks Kraft p. 21; Corbis/CNP p. 18 (Ron
Sachs); Corbis/The Denver Post pp. 38 & 39 (Peter
Turnley); Corbis/In Visu pp. 6, 36, 44 & 50 (Jérome
Sessini), 28 & 34 (Olivier Coret), 33 (Antoine Serra), 40
(Christophe Calais); Corbis/Sygma pp. 14 (UNSCOM),
17, 20; Popperfoto.com pp. 9, 12, 13; Topham/AP
pp. 4, 11; Topham/Image Works p. 24; Topham/Photri
pp. 42, 46; Topham/UPPA Ltd pp. 10, 25.

Cover photograph of an American soldier carrying an
unexploded shell in Baghdad in May 2003 reproduced
with permission of Reuters/Faleh Kheiber

The publishers would like to thank Bob Rees, historian
and assistant head teacher, for his assistance in the
preparation of this book.

Every effort has been made to contact copyright
holders of any material reproduced in this book. Any
omissions will be rectified in subsequent printings if
notice is given to the publishers.

The paper used to print this book comes from
sustainable resources.

Words appearing in the text in bold, **like this,** are explained in the glossary.

Contents

Introduction

In March 2003 the US and British governments took the controversial decision to send their troops into the Middle Eastern country of Iraq. The resulting war, which was fought wholly inside Iraq, lasted just over three weeks. It ended – at least in the sense that fighting on a large scale ended – when the invaders' main objective, the overthrow of the Iraqi government led by Saddam Hussein, was achieved.

During those three weeks, around 5000 Iraqis – roughly half of them civilians – and 158 US and British troops were killed. US forces fired 750 **cruise missiles**, and the Anglo-American air forces **coalition** flew over 30,000 **sorties**. Enormous damage was done to Iraq's economic **infrastructure** – its buildings, communications, transport system and power supplies.

A general view of Baghdad before the 2003 war. Note the poster of Saddam Hussein in the bottom left-hand corner.

The background

The war in 2003 was the last in a series of wars involving Iraq and its leader of over 30 years, Saddam Hussein. In 1980 he launched an aggressive war against neighbouring Iran, a war that lasted nine years. During those years he received considerable financial and military aid from both **Western** countries and other **Arab** states. The war eventually ended in stalemate, with Iraq virtually **bankrupt**, and so in August 1990 Saddam sought to recover his losses by invading oil-rich

Kuwait. Six months later he was ejected by an US-led, **United Nations**-authorized, coalition of armies in the **Gulf War**.

Iraq was ordered to give up whatever **nuclear**, **chemical** and **biological weapons** it possessed, and to abandon the idea of building any more. **Economic sanctions** were imposed when the international community suspected that Iraq was not complying with this order. **No-fly zones** were enforced over southern and northern Iraq to prevent Saddam using air power against his own people. Twelve years of hardship followed for most of the Iraqi people, twelve years in which Saddam was kept weak by his country's poverty and the constant threat of US and British air attacks. He obviously posed a threat to his own terrorized people, but few believed, at the beginning of the 21st century, that he posed any real threat to the outside world.

For and against

Then came September 11, 2001 and the **terrorist** attacks on the World Trade Center in New York, and the Pentagon in Washington, which launched the **War on Terrorism**, and USA's decision to go after Saddam as part of that war. The British supported their transatlantic **ally**, but many other prominent states, like France and Germany did not, and the eventual decision to invade Iraq divided both the international community and many national communities. Enormous protests around the world reflected widespread doubts about the legality, morality and wisdom of such an invasion. While its supporters saw it as part of a righteous war on terrorism, many of its opponents saw it as either a terrible mistake or a sordid grab for glory and oil.

Once the war was over, few were sorry to be rid of Saddam. But many still doubted the wisdom of overthrowing him in such a manner, without international agreement or support, and with little notion of what the long-term consequences would be for Iraq, the Middle East and the world. What is certain is that those consequences, whatever they are, will shape international relations for a long time to come.

How do we know?

Someone who wants to understand an event, or series of events, that took place in the past usually makes for a library or a bookshop, and looks for a book on that subject. But if the event in question – like the war in Iraq – is very recent then the number of books available may be limited.

The other obvious source of information is the news **media**. Many newspapers, radio programmes and TV programmes offer a day-by-day breakdown of what is happening in the world, describing events and trying to make sense of them for their readers, listeners and viewers. Many libraries keep their newspapers for weeks or even months, while both broadcasters and newspapers have internet sites which allow people to access their output in the recent past. Books, too, can be useful. They may not cover the events in question, but they can provide the background to those events, and make them easier to understand.

Primary and secondary sources

All sources of information are either **primary sources** or **secondary sources**. Primary sources are the written or spoken accounts of people who played some part in, or were witnesses to, the events concerned. They could be eyewitnesses or decision makers, those who made it happen or those it happened to. Secondary sources are accounts which make use of primary sources, but which are put together by those who were not directly involved. They attempt to paint a fuller picture, one which sees things from all points of view rather than just one.

A truck driver, on his way out of Iraq during the early days of the war, is questioned at the border by waiting journalists. To historians, whatever information he passes on to the journalists is a primary source.

Neither source should ever be taken at face value. Individuals always have a partial view of events, and this view will be further coloured by their own self-interest, beliefs and prejudices. And the historian who tries to disentangle the facts from the wishful thinking will have his or her own beliefs and prejudices. Every picture is distorted, but some are more distorted than others.

Working out which is which is often difficult, particularly where recent events are concerned. Some newspapers and broadcasting companies are **biased** in favour of their own countries, and most reflect a particular set of political opinions.

An Iraqi newspaper carrying news of the death of Saddam's sons Qusay and Uday, 29 July 2003. Reports in newspapers are just one source of information used by historians to try to build a picture or account of an important event.

Armed with whatever background information he or she can gather, the reader, listener or viewer must try to read between the lines, to separate opinion from fact.

Telling the story of the war

This book uses both a secondary source – an historian's account – and a wide selection of primary sources to explore the background, events and aftermath of the 2003 war in Iraq. Some of the primary sources, like the US soldier on page 39, fought in the war, or, like the family on page 29, were victims of it. Others, like the leaders quoted on pages 19 and 21, took the decisions that made it happen. All have their point of view, but some also have a point to prove. By putting them all together, we gain a clearer picture of where the war came from, how it was fought, and what its outcome is likely to be.

Iraq

Before World War I, what is now Iraq was part of the Turkish **Ottoman Empire**. At the end of World War I the empire collapsed, and its three most south-easterly provinces were joined to form the state of Iraq. They were populated by diverse **ethnic** and religious groups, a diversity that has proved a source of many problems in Iraq.

The population of Iraq is roughly 75 per cent **Arab** and 18 per cent **Kurd**, with the remainder made up of several much smaller groups. Ninety-five per cent of all Iraqis are **Muslims**. Of these, 60 per cent are **Shi'a Muslims** and 40 percent, which includes all the Kurds, are **Sunni Muslims**. The Iraqi population is therefore made up of three basic groups: the Sunni Kurds in the north, the Sunni Arabs in the north and centre, and the Shi'a Arabs in the centre and south.

Map showing part of the present-day Middle East.

For its first twelve years, Iraq was ruled by the British. The Turks had favoured their fellow-Sunnis in Iraq, and the British found it convenient to rely on them also. They brought in an Arabian Sunni to become Iraq's first King – Faisal I – and saw to it that the local Sunni **elite** continued to hold most of the key positions in the local government and economy. The country was given official independence in 1932, but the British continued to hold the real power. It was only in 1958 that British influence was finally ended by a military **coup**.

Many of the coup's supporters came from the **Arab nationalist Ba'ath** Party, but the next two governments were led by non-Ba'athist generals. In 1968 the Ba'ath Party finally took power for itself through another coup. The party's little-known but powerful deputy secretary-general was a 31-year-old Sunni Muslim named Saddam Hussein.

The moment of change

Iraq only received real independence in 1958, when the Iraqi **Free Officers** overthrew the British-backed monarchy and government. In this newspaper report, a British eyewitness describes some of the key events.

Mrs Carol Magee, wife of a British major, who lived near the palace (in Baghdad), described the assassination [sudden killing] of members of the royal family. She said: 'The rebels moved field **artillery** to bear on the royal palace and shouted for the King and his household to come out.'

The King and members of his household, including (his uncle) the Crown Prince emerged into the palace gardens. The rebel platoon commander ordered everyone to come with him. The Crown Prince replied that they would not move; he said that the rebels had no authority. He then ordered his escort to open fire, and the rebel commander was shot dead. According to Mrs Magee, carnage followed, and all 19 of the royal party fell dead. Terrible things happened afterwards, including the mutilation of the Crown Prince's body and the hanging up of the corpse.

Mrs Magee understood that (Prime Minister) Nuri es Said escaped through a passage leading to the river, where he boarded a boat. He was caught a few hours later wearing a woman's black robe.

In the aftermath of the 1958 coup demonstrators carry pictures of new leader General Kassem and placards demanding the death sentence for members of the previous **regime**.

Saddam and Iraq

Within weeks of the **Ba'ath** Party's takeover in 1968, Saddam Hussein had established himself as the most powerful man in Iraq. Ahmad al Bakr was the president, but Saddam, who became the official vice-president in 1969, controlled the **security police** and many other government departments, all of which he filled with family members, friends and other supporters. His was the voice that counted.

An official portrait of Saddam Hussein in 1977.

There was no attempt to introduce **democracy**. Saddam was supposed to represent the Ba'ath Party, but instead the members of that party became representatives of Saddam. These Ba'ath Party members were used by Saddam to put his orders into practice. Disagreeing with Saddam was not tolerated – anyone who opposed him was likely to be arrested, tortured, and either killed or imprisoned. The Iraqi **media**, which he completely controlled, was used to build up his image as the father of the nation and a hero to Arabs everywhere.

There was some justification for this praise, at least until 1980. During his first decade in power Saddam did bring great benefits to the Iraqi people. He took Iraq's oil industry away from the foreign companies that had always controlled it, and used the country's rapidly rising income – the 1970s was a decade of soaring world oil prices – to benefit the country. He started new industries, brought electricity to rural communities, improved education and health care, and set up unemployment pay and pensions. Women were encouraged to do jobs which had previously been forbidden to them. Saddam was a **Muslim**, but not a Muslim **fundamentalist**. He believed that **Islam** should adapt to the modern world.

Saddam Hussein on educating the young

Saddam Hussein's Iraq was similar in many ways to other **totalitarian** societies, in that it put the interests of the state above those of individuals. Here, in an extract from a speech to a mass meeting of Iraqi Ministry of Education employees in 1976, Saddam Hussein insists on two things: firstly, that children must learn to put loyalty to the Party before loyalty to their families, and secondly, that they are taught an instinctive distrust of foreigners.

Teach students to object to their parents if they hear them discussing state secrets, and to warn them that this is not correct. Teach them to criticize their mothers and fathers, respectfully, if they hear them talking about organizational and Ba'ath Party secrets. You must place a son of the revolution with a trustworthy eye and firm mind in every corner, and teach him to object, with respect, to either of his parents should he discover them wasting the state's wealth, which he should let them know is dearer than his own... Also teach the child at this stage to beware of the foreigner, for the foreigner is a pair of eyes for his own country and some of them are **saboteurs** of our revolution. Therefore, accompanying foreigners and talking with them in the absence of known controls [unsupervised by Ba'ath Party members] is forbidden.

Iraqi folk dancers perform at the Saddam Stadium in Baghdad, 1984. The **propaganda** poster shows Saddam himself surrounded by adoring children.

Saddam and his neighbours

In 1979 a revolution in neighbouring Iran brought **Shi'a Muslim fundamentalists** to power. These fundamentalists were profoundly anti-**Western**; they believed that Western-style modernization and ideas were undermining **Islamic** principles and the traditional **Muslim** way of life. They were particularly angered by Western insistence on improved rights for women and what they saw as a Western neglect of religious values in favour of material progress. Faced with the hostility of these fundamentalists, Western powers like the USA looked for **allies** among **Arab** modernizers like Saddam. For the moment, Saddam's value as an opponent of Iran was considered more important than the well-known brutality of his **regime**.

In 1980 Saddam went to war with Iran. He did so for two reasons: he was afraid that the Iranian fundamentalists would provoke a Shi'a rebellion in southern Iraq, and, he wanted to get his hands on Iran's oil. The USA and its allies – particularly **Sunni Muslim** Saudi Arabia and Kuwait – encouraged and helped him throughout the eight-year war. In particular, Saddam received significant help from the West in developing what became known as **weapons of mass destruction**. He was given **nuclear** technology by France, and **chemical** warfare materials by the USA, Italy and Germany.

The Iran-Iraq war ended without a clear winner, but **bankrupted** Iraq. Iraq owed billions of dollars to Kuwait and Saudi Arabia, and since Iraq had fought the war at least partly on their behalf Saddam expected them to cancel the debt. When they refused, he decided to restore Iraq's finances by invading Kuwait and seizing its enormous oil wealth.

Revolution in neighbouring Iran in 1979: a crowd outside Tehran University welcomes home the country's new fundamentalist leader, Ayatollah Khomeini.

Halabja

Saddam Hussein's regime used chemical weapons against both Iranian troops and its opponents within Iraq itself. Eyewitness reports of the March 1988 attack on the **Kurdish** town of Halabja, and the villages which surrounded it, were included in a US government report on the incident.

As described by the villagers, the bombs that fell on the morning of August 25 did not produce a large explosion. Only a weak sound could be heard and then a yellowish cloud spread out from the centre of the explosion and became a thin mist. The air became filled with a mixture of smells – 'bad garlic', 'rotten onions', and 'bad apples'.

Those who were very close to the bombs died almost instantly. Those who did not die instantly found it difficult to breathe and began to vomit. The gas stung their eyes, skin and lungs... Many suffered temporary blindness. Those who could not run from the growing smell, mostly the very old, the very young, died.

Ahmad Mohammed, a Kurd, recalled that day. 'My mother and father were burnt; they just died and turned black.' Bashir Shemessidin testified: 'In our village, 200 to 300 people died. All the trees dried up. It smelled like something burned. The whole world turned yellow.'

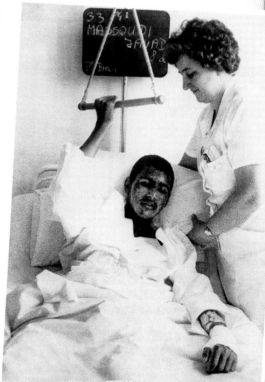

June 1983: an Iranian soldier lies in hospital after suffering burns during an Iraqi chemical weapons attack during the Iran-Iraq War.

War and containment

The attack on Kuwait in August 1990 proved a huge miscalculation. Saddam had expected the world to protest, but to do nothing. Instead, a large **coalition** of countries was put together under the **UN** flag and US leadership, and in the **Gulf War** of February 1991 his forces were driven out. Around 100,000 Iraqi people became casualties in this war, but Saddam himself survived. There was no UN **authorization** to topple his **regime**, and the **Arab** states in the coalition were unwilling to see an Arab government overthrown. So when the **Shi'as** in the south and the **Kurds** in the north both rose in rebellion against Saddam, the coalition forces refused to help in his overthrow. It was only after thousands of Shi'as and Kurds had been killed that the USA and British air forces intervened to enforce '**no-fly zones**' in the north and south, and thus prevent Saddam from killing still more.

UN weapons inspectors at work in Iraq during the 1990s.

By the terms of the peace, Saddam agreed to stop his **nuclear**, **chemical** and **biological weapons** programmes, and to destroy any such weapons which he possessed. He agreed to allow UN weapons inspectors to verify that he was keeping his word. Until they could do so, his country would be subject to **economic sanctions**. It could sell a certain amount of oil to buy food and medicines, but that was all. Through enforcement of these inspections and sanctions, the coalition powers hoped to '**contain**' Saddam and to prevent him from becoming a threat to his neighbours again.

Over the next seven years Saddam made things as difficult as he could for the inspectors, and in 1998, they withdrew from Iraq. His unhelpful attitude convinced many **Western** leaders and UN inspectors that he still had something to hide, and that he would produce new weapons if given the chance to do so. The sanctions continued.

Interview with a weapons inspector

Former US Marine Scott Ritter led a UN weapons inspection team in Iraq. Unlike many of his colleagues, Ritter believed that the policy of containment continued to work after the withdrawal of the inspectors in 1998. In this interview given in September 2002 he explained why this was so, and why he was convinced that Iraq posed no imminent threat to its neighbours or the rest of the world.

No weapons inspections team has set foot in Iraq since 1998. I think Iraq was technically capable of restarting its chemical weapon manufacturing programmes within six months of our departure. That leaves three and a half years for Iraq to have manufactured and weaponized [turned into weapons] all the horrors that the Bush [US president] administration claims as motivations [reasons] for an attack. The important phrase here, however, is 'technically capable'. If no one were watching, Iraq could do this. But just as with the nuclear and biological weapons programmes, they would have to start from scratch, having been deprived of all equipment, facilities and research. They would have to import the complicated tools and technology required, and this would be detected. The manufacture of chemical weapons gives off gases that would have been detected by now if they existed. We have been watching, via satellite and other means, and have seen none of this. If Iraq were producing weapons today, we would have definitive proof, plain and simple.

The rise of the US neo-conservatives

During the 1990s a group of influential US politicians known as the **neo-conservatives** came to prominence. This group included men like Donald Rumsfeld, Dick Cheney, Paul Wolfowitz and Richard Perle, most of whom had served in previous **Republican** governments. They argued that the end of the **Cold War** – and the USA's emergence as the world's only **superpower** – presented the USA with a great opportunity to re-write the international rule book and spread American values of **democracy** and **free enterprise** to the rest of the world.

They believed the US had not been decisive enough during the **Gulf War**, that its forces should have overthrown Saddam, whatever the **UN** or the **coalition** partners had said. They wanted to remove Saddam from power, using military force if necessary. They urged this policy on the **Democrat** President Bill Clinton in a series of speeches, articles and letters, but Clinton made no attempt to remove Saddam.

When George W. Bush became president in 2001, many neo-conservatives got important jobs in his government. Dick Cheney became vice-president, while Donald Rumsfeld and Paul Wolfowitz were appointed to the two top jobs at the defence department. Other members of the Bush government, like Secretary of State Colin Powell, were more reluctant to adopt the neo-conservative go-it-alone approach, and more willing to work with the US's traditional international partners. President Bush himself seemed torn between the two. What persuaded him to accept the neo-conservative arguments were the **terrorist** attacks on 11 September 2001.

The twin towers of the World Trade Center in New York City just after they were struck by hijacked airliners on 11 September 2001.

A call for action

In January 1998 a group of American neo-conservatives, including Donald Rumsfeld and Paul Wolfowitz, sent a published letter to President Clinton. In it, they urged him to take decisive action against Saddam Hussein and Iraq.

If Saddam acquires the capability to deliver **weapons of mass destruction**, as he is almost certain to do, then the safety of American troops in the region, the safety of our friends and **allies** like Israel and the moderate **Arab** states, and a significant portion of the world's oil supply, will all be put at risk.

Donald Rumsfeld, the US secretary of defense during the 2003 war in Iraq.

The only acceptable strategy is one that eliminates this possibility. In the short term, this means a willingness to undertake military action, as diplomacy [talking between governments] is clearly failing. In the long term it means removing Saddam Hussein and his **regime** from power. That now needs to become the aim of American foreign policy [the goals that govern how the nation interacts with other nations].

Although we are fully aware of the dangers and difficulties of implementing this policy, we believe the dangers of failing to do so are greater. We believe the US has the authority under existing **UN resolutions** to take the necessary steps, including military steps, to protect our interests in the Gulf. In any case, American policy cannot continue to be crippled by a misguided insistence on unanimity [complete agreement] in the UN **Security Council**.

After September 11

The attacks of 11 September 2001 were carried out by the **al-Qaeda terrorist** organization, based in Afghanistan. On 17 September, as the first step in America's **War on Terrorism**, President George W. Bush agreed on a plan for the invasion of Afghanistan. On the same day he asked the defence department to draw up plans for an invasion of Iraq, even though Iraq had not been involved in the attacks.

President George W. Bush addresses the American people in a televised broadcast after the terrorist attacks of 11 September, 2001.

By January 2002 Afghanistan had been occupied and al-Qaeda scattered. In his **State of the Union address** to **Congress** that month, Bush accused Iraq, Iran and North Korea of forming an 'Axis of Evil' that threatened world peace. In another speech in June, he said that the USA would take **pre-emptive** action against such states – that is, it would attack them first if it seemed they intended to attack the USA or any of its **allies**. By this time the Bush government had made it clear that Iraq would be the first target of this new policy. The only question was whether the government would be satisfied with forcing Saddam to disarm, or would insist on removing him from power.

There was widespread international agreement that something needed to be done about Saddam, but disagreement over exactly what. The British government supported the US position that action was urgently needed, while other important states, like France, Germany, Russia and China argued that **containment** could still work. In September Saddam tried to ward off an attack by agreeing to the return of the **UN** weapons inspectors. Over the next few months the inspectors searched for Iraq's **weapons of mass destruction**, but were unable to either prove or disprove their existence. In the meantime, the US and British governments began building up their military forces in neighbouring Kuwait.

Axis of Evil

George W. Bush's State of the Union address on 29 January 2002 provides a good example of a **primary source** which can be interpreted in very different ways. Supporters of the government pointed out that the horrors of September 11 were still fresh in American minds, and that the president was simply reflecting the American peoples' demand that something drastic had to done. Opponents pointed out that the president offered a completely one-sided view of events. He made no mention, for example, of the fact that the USA has more weapons of mass destruction than any other nation.

We must prevent the terrorists and **regimes** who seek **chemical**, **biological** or **nuclear weapons** from threatening the United States and the world. . . Some of these regimes have been pretty quiet since September the 11th. But we know their true nature. North Korea is a regime arming with missiles and weapons of mass destruction. . . Iran aggressively pursues these weapons and exports terror. . . Iraq continues to flaunt its hostility toward America and to support terror.

States like these, and their terrorist allies, make up an Axis of Evil, arming to threaten the peace of the world. By seeking weapons of mass destruction, these regimes pose a grave and growing danger. They could provide these arms to terrorists. They could attack our allies or attempt to blackmail the United States.

I will not wait on events, while dangers gather. I will not stand by, as peril draws closer and closer. The United States will not permit the world's most dangerous regimes to threaten us with the world's most destructive weapons.

The case for military action

The argument for military action was mainly put by the US and British governments. Some other governments, like those of Spain and Italy, supported them, and so did many individuals around the world. In most countries, however, a majority opposed the war.

There were several strands to the pro-war argument. Saddam had supported **terrorism** by giving money to the families of Palestinian **suicide bombers**, and he was supposedly developing **weapons of mass destruction**. There was a risk that he could hand such weapons over to terrorists, who might then launch attacks on the **West**. Secondly, by continuing his attempt to create weapons of mass destruction, Saddam was deliberately flouting many **UN resolutions**. Allowing him to do this would undermine the authority of the UN. Thirdly, Saddam was head of a brutal **regime**, which had tortured and killed many of its own people, and invaded two other countries, Iran and Kuwait. The world would be a better place without him.

In addition, the creation of a new, **democratic** Iraq would encourage other Middle Eastern states to become more democratic and open, and more friendly to the West. This would be good for the people of the region, who would be freer and more prosperous. It would also help the West, because the region's oil, on which the West so much depended, would then be in safer, friendlier hands.

Iraqi President Saddam Hussein at a meeting with his military advisers before the war in 2003.

Tony Blair addresses the House of Commons

On 24 September 2002 British prime minister, Tony Blair, spoke to an emergency session of the House of Commons. Earlier that day his government had published a **dossier**, which sought to prove that Saddam posed a real and imminent threat. Several of the 'facts' quoted in the dossier and in this speech, were disputed at the time.

At any time Saddam could have cooperated with the United Nations. But he didn't. Why?

The dossier we publish today gives the answer. The reason is – his **chemical**, **biological** and **nuclear weapons** programme is active, detailed and growing. The policy of **containment** is not working. The weapons of mass destruction programme is not shut down. It is up and running.

The Joint Intelligence Committee [which prepared the dossier] concludes that Iraq has chemical and biological weapons, that Saddam has continued to produce them, that he has existing and active

British Prime Minister Tony Blair was the staunchest supporter of George W. Bush's decision to go to war with Iraq.

military plans for the use of chemical and biological weapons, which could be activated within forty-five minutes, and that he is actively trying to acquire nuclear weapons.

Let me put it at its simplest. With this man Saddam, with this detailed intelligence, with what we know and what we can reasonably guess – would the world be wise to leave things as they are, to say that we should do nothing?

The case against military action

Opposition to military action came in two basic forms. Pacifists – those who oppose all violence – argued that there was always a better way to deal with disputes. However, most of those who were against this war were prepared to take military action against Saddam, but only once all the other ways of bringing him to heel had been exhausted. They wanted the **UN** weapons inspectors to be given time to do their job, and to prove whether or not Saddam really did have **weapons of mass destruction**.

Opponents of military action included the governments of France, Germany, Russia and many other countries, and large proportions of the populations of most countries, including the USA and UK. They argued that there was a clear majority in the UN in favour of waiting for weapons inspectors to finish their work and that the US and UK would undermine UN authority if they went to war on their own. They argued that a **pre-emptive** attack would be illegal, and would set a terrible precedent.

Anti-war demonstrators in Paris, March 2003. The placard demands a lifting of the **economic sanctions** against Iraq.

Few disputed that Saddam's **regime** was brutal, that he had flouted countless **UN resolutions,** or that he had aided **terrorists**. But other regimes were just as brutal, or had flouted as many UN resolutions. And Saddam had never had any links with **Muslim fundamentalist** terrorists like **al-Qaeda**. It seemed to most opponents of military action that the US and Britain were picking on Iraq because they needed to show the world who was boss, and were eager to secure control over Iraq's enormous oil reserves.

An author speaks out

John Le Carré is a well-known author of political and spy fiction. On 15 January 2003 *The Times* printed his article 'The United States of America has gone mad.' In it, he reflected the opinions of many who were bitterly opposed to the coming war.

THE TIMES

15 January 2003

How Bush and his administration succeeded in deflecting [turning aside] America's anger from Osama bin Laden [the leader of al-Qaeda] to Saddam Hussein is one of the great public relations conjuring tricks of history. But they swung it. A recent poll tells us that one in two Americans now believe that Saddam was responsible for the attack on the World Trade Center. But the American public is not merely being misled. It is being browbeaten and kept in a state of ignorance and fear.

What is at stake is not an Axis of Evil – but oil, money and people's lives... If Saddam didn't have the oil, he could torture his citizens to his heart's content. Other leaders do it every day – think Saudi Arabia, think Pakistan, think Turkey, think Syria, think Egypt.

Baghdad represents no clear and present danger to its neighbours, and none to the US or Britain. Saddam's weapons of mass destruction, if he's still got them, will be peanuts by comparison with the stuff America could hurl at him at five minutes' notice.

The UN **Security Council** discusses the arguments for and against military action in Iraq, 7 March 2003.

The decision is taken

The arguments over military action came to a head in late February and early March 2003. The weapons inspectors had found some evidence of illegal Iraqi weapon development, but nothing which suggested that Iraq posed an imminent threat to its neighbours, let alone the rest of the world. Despite this, the USA and Britain argued that action to disarm Iraq by force was now urgent. Their opponents believed that they were eager to complete their military campaign before the intense heat of the Iraqi summer made conditions too difficult for fighting.

As war grew nearer, huge protest demonstrations took place around the world. In the **UN** a majority of states argued that a new **UN resolution** was needed to **authorize** the use of force against Saddam, and the British government, knowing that many of its citizens would only support a war which had UN backing, agreed to seek such a resolution. It soon became clear that there was no majority for such a resolution, and that the French, and perhaps the Russians, would **veto** any resolution authorizing military action before the inspectors had completed their work. The US and UK governments then decided that they would go to war without further UN authorization. In Britain, several government ministers resigned in protest.

The USA and UK received political backing from several other nations, and the word '**coalition**' was used to describe the forces involved, as had been the case in the **Gulf War** of 1991. This time, however, the military forces were almost exclusively American and British.

A US peace rally in Albuquerque, New Mexico, USA. This was one of many such events held across the world on 18 January 2003.

Robin Cook's resignation speech

The highest-ranking British minister to resign in protest against the war was Robin Cook, Leader of the House of Commons and former foreign secretary. On 18 March 2003 he explained his reasons to the House of Commons.

Britain is being asked to embark on a war without agreement in any of the international bodies of which we are a leading partner – not **NATO**, not the **European Union** and, now, not the United Nations **Security Council**. The US can afford to go it alone, but Britain is not a **superpower**. Our interests are best protected not by unilateral [one-sided] action but by multilateral [many-sided] agreement and a world order governed by rules…

Robin Cook explains his resignation from Tony Blair's government in protest against the decision to go to war.

On Iraq, I believe the prevailing mood of the British people is sound. They do not doubt that Saddam is a brutal dictator, but they are not persuaded that he is a clear and present danger to Britain. They want inspections to be given a chance, and they suspect that they are being pushed too quickly into conflict by a US administration with an agenda of its own. Above all, they are uneasy at Britain going out on a limb on a military adventure without a broader international coalition, and against the hostility of many of our traditional **allies**.

I intend to join those who will vote against military action now. It is for that reason that I resign from the government.

The opposing forces

The number of US and British forces in the Gulf region had been steadily increasing since the summer of 2002, and by 20 March 2003, the day war began, there were some 130,000 ground troops poised to invade Iraq. These troops were equipped with the most modern tanks and armoured vehicles, and supported by the most technologically advanced air forces and communication systems that the world had ever seen. The USA accounts for over 40 per cent of global military spending, and the force gathered to overthrow Saddam Hussein reflected its enormous superiority over any other single armed force in the world.

On paper, there were probably between two and three Iraqis in uniform for every **coalition** soldier, but their weapons, tanks and communication systems were old and their air force virtually non-existent. They only had a few short-range missiles, which had been successfully concealed from coalition spy-planes.

The US and British armies were made up of well-trained, professional soldiers, most of whom believed that they were fighting to liberate the Iraqi people from a cruel dictator, and to make the world a safer place. The Iraqi Army, by contrast, was mostly composed of unwilling conscripts – people who had been ordered to join the armed forces by their government. No doubt some of them resented the invasion of their country, but few had any burning desire to fight or die for Saddam Hussein. The War in Iraq was, in every respect, a profoundly unequal contest.

The Guardian

February 2003

Morale was very low, Abbas said, both among his fellow conscripts and among civilians. 'We want America to attack because of the bad situation in our country. But we don't want America to launch air strikes against Iraqi soldiers because we are forced to shoot and defend. We are also victims of the situation.'

Conditions back in the Iraqi trenches were not so good, he said. 'We have two blankets for every soldier, but they are very thin and don't keep us warm. The officers beat us. And the food is disgusting. I'm only paid 50 dinars [about £3] a month.'

'There are two groups in the Iraqi army', Abbas said. 'The Republican Guard will support and defend Saddam. The ordinary soldiers and many of the commanders will surrender.'

A well-equipped US soldier in Kuwait gets his equipment ready on the eve of the ground war, 20 March 2003.

War from the air

The first attack of the war, in the early hours of 20 March, was a number of **cruise missiles** fired simultaneously from US ships in the Persian Gulf at government targets in the Iraqi capital, Baghdad. Before the war started, US military leaders announced that they would launch an air assault devastating enough to 'shock and awe', but most inhabitants of Baghdad were unaffected by these early strikes, and by those that followed over the next few days. Relying on the much-improved accuracy of their 'smart' bombs – bombs guided to their target by laser or radio – the US and British military concentrated on precision attacks against government and military targets, taking care to minimize casualties among the civilian population.

There were two reasons for this. Firstly, it made sense to attack such targets – it was Saddam and his army who needed scaring into surrender, not the Iraqi people. Secondly, the widespread unpopularity of the war made it important to limit civilian casualties and Britain and the US needed to be seen to be doing this so they could build up international support.

Outside Baghdad, in the smaller towns and countryside of Iraq, the world's **media** was much thinner on the ground, and air attacks may have been targeted with less care. More importantly from the military point of view, the **coalition** air forces relentlessly pounded the Iraqi troops wherever they found them. These attacks inevitably resulted in heavy casualties.

Report from Baghdad

Subhy Haddad is a BBC World Service reporter who lives in Iraq and reported from Baghdad during the war. Here are his thoughts as he and his family waited for the nightly bombing to begin.

In Baghdad at the moment, as the sun sets, those who are living in apartments or on high floors come straight down and find somewhere to spend the night on the ground floor. Some people have cellars and spend the night there. Those who can afford to leave Baghdad try to find a place on the outskirts of the city – they just jump in their cars and leave the city for the night.

Children, especially those who witnessed the 1998 bombings – are so scared. My own eldest child is 11 years old, she is scared to death. In 1998 one of the missiles fell about half a kilometre [0.3 miles] away and broke some of our windows. From that day on she has been in such a condition you cannot imagine it. When she is asleep and hears a door banging she wakes up shouting. This is my own daughter, but other children are the same.

Now the streets are deserted. You cannot hear cars, or people – they are all in their houses waiting for the missiles to begin... Sorry, my wife is shouting, the bombardment has started. This time the raid has started before the air-raid siren. The windows are shaking. I have to go.

'Shock and awe': Baghdad under air attack from cruise missiles on the second day of the war, 21 March 2003.

Advances on the ground

The original plan had been to enter Iraq from both north and south, but Turkey's late refusal to allow attacks from its territory ruled this out. Instead, the **coalition** armies crossed over from Kuwait early in the morning of 20 March. There were three major forces involved. On the right, British forces with some American support moved north and north-east towards Iraq's second-largest city, Basra, and the al-Faw Peninsula. Their main aims were to capture the southern oilfields and Iraq's ports. In the centre, US Marines moved north towards the Rumeilah oilfield and the Tigris valley. On the left, a second US army headed by the 3rd Infantry Division headed north-west across the desert towards the Euphrates valley. The ultimate objective of both US armies was Baghdad.

The US and British met little resistance in these first few days. The al-Faw Peninsula was taken and Basra surrounded. By Sunday 23 March, US forces were in the vicinity of Najaf, two-thirds of the way to Baghdad. It seemed as if the war would be over quickly.

But then, over the next few days, the advance slowed to a virtual halt. There were several reasons for this: difficulty in keeping the forward units supplied, unusually fierce sandstorms and the beginnings of Iraqi resistance – generally speaking, the best Iraqi troops had been deployed in the centre of the country, around Baghdad. In Euphrates valley towns like Nasiriyah and Najaf, the US troops found themselves under serious attack for the first time. When it came to urban street-fighting their technological superiority and air support counted for less, and worries were expressed about what might be waiting for them in Baghdad.

Map showing main lines of **coalition** attack into Iraq, March–April 2003.

An eyewitness account of the fighting

BBC TV journalist Clive Myrie was **'embedded'** with 40 Commando, a unit of the Royal Marines. Here, on the first full day of the war, he gives an eyewitness account of their attack on the al-Faw Peninsula in the far south of Iraq.

Iraqi bunker positions were being spotted all the time. 'Psy Ops', or Psychological Operations, were then called in. A marine carrying a heavy backpack with a loudspeaker attached would flip the 'on' switch of a tape recorder and the words 'you're surrounded, surrender, you won't be harmed' would boom out in Arabic.

On one occasion we watched from a distance as this scenario was played out. The Iraqis in their bunker didn't budge. In fact they fired back. The British called in a **mortar** attack and the bunker was mercilessly shelled. When it was thought safe we went to look at the damage. There were bodies everywhere. I counted six, and one man dying on the ground. Royal Marine medics rushed over and tried to save him. As a civilian watching all this it was a strange sight, because minutes earlier the marines had been trying to kill him...

Iraqis in other bunker positions knew what was going on and decided it wasn't worth fighting anymore. Within three or four hours of the first marines landing on al-Faw, Iraq's troops began to surrender.

US soldiers of the 101st Airborne Division in Najaf, 30 March 2003. They are looking for Iraqi soldiers who had been launching mortar shells at US army positions.

Civilian casualties

During the days in which their ground advance was stalled, the **coalition** was also hit by accusations that it was causing unacceptable civilian casualties. One incident in particular, the bombing of a Baghdad marketplace on 26 March, which killed around twenty civilians and seriously wounded many more, made the headlines in newspapers and TV news around the world. Two days later another marketplace bombing, resulting in more than 50 deaths, received equally wide coverage. There were further horrifying stories of civilian victims: a boy who lost both arms, a dead baby on a pavement, cars full of families destroyed as they tried to escape the fighting in Nasiriyah.

Such stories reinforced the opinions of those who opposed the war, and forced supporters of the war on to the defensive. The coalition's political and military authorities claimed that the Iraqis had placed military installations close to civilian areas, and that, in any case, some civilian casualties were inevitable in any war. But they insisted that they were doing their best to limit them, and the evidence suggests that they were fairly successful in doing so. One independent source put the number of civilians killed in the war at around 2300. It was of course no comfort to the dead or their families, but this was, by the standards of previous wars, an astonishingly low figure.

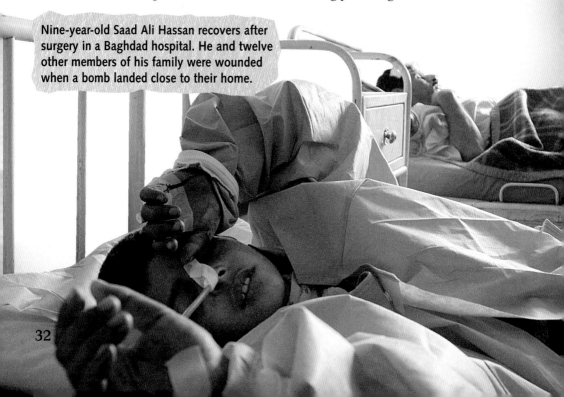

Nine-year-old Saad Ali Hassan recovers after surgery in a Baghdad hospital. He and twelve other members of his family were wounded when a bomb landed close to their home.

A marketplace in the Al Chaab area of Baghdad after two US missiles exploded killing around twenty people and wounding many more. At the time of the bombing Baghdad was also hit by a sandstorm that covered the city in a cloud of red dust.

Robert Fisk describes the aftermath of a bombing

Many **Western** reporters remained in Baghdad throughout the war. Here one of them, Robert Fisk of the British newspaper the *Independent*, vividly describes what he saw and heard in the Baghdad marketplace bombed on 26 March.

The Independent

March 2003

It was an outrage, an obscenity... Two missiles from an American jet killed . . . by my estimate, more than twenty Iraqi civilians, torn to pieces before they could be 'liberated'; by the nation that destroyed their lives. Who dares, I ask myself, to call this 'collateral damage' [military jargon to describe civilian casualties of the war]?

Abu Taleb Street was packed with pedestrians and motorists when the American pilot approached through the dense sandstorm that covered northern Baghdad in a cloak of red and yellow dust and rain yesterday morning. It's a dirt-poor neighbourhood of mostly **Shi'a Muslims**, a place of oil-sodden cars, repair shops, overcrowded apartments and cheap cafés. Everyone I spoke to heard the plane. One man, so shocked by the headless corpses he had just seen, could say only two words. 'Roar, flash' he kept saying and then closed his eyes so tight that the muscles rippled between them.

The media and the war

The war in Iraq was the most reported war in history. Foreign journalists remained in Baghdad throughout the war, and managed – despite restrictions on their movements and what they were allowed to say – to paint a remarkable picture of a capital under attack. Another seven hundred journalists were permanently attached to different **coalition** units. These **embedded** journalists had a front seat to the shooting war, but their movement and speech were also limited. And as they shared in the dangers facing the troops, it was hard for them not to see things from the coalition's point of view.

Other journalists preferred the freedom of operating independently, a choice which often proved dangerous. Almost all of the thirteen journalists killed during the war – most of them by **friendly fire** – were operating independently.

Much of the **media** coverage was inaccurate. The government-controlled Iraqi media made no attempt to tell the truth, and the increasingly outrageous lies of Saeed al-Sharaf, Iraq's information minister, turned him into an international joke. The US and British media was also prone to exaggeration: Saddam's death was reported on several occasions, and towns were said to have been captured when this was clearly not the case. In the USA in particular, it was rare to see pictures of the war's victims.

The only visual media outlets which fairly reflected both sides of the conflict, and which were willing to show their viewers the human cost of the war, came from those nations that were not directly involved.

Bloggers

During the war several ordinary residents of Baghdad filed regular reports on the internet or 'weblogs'. Since their voices were not official voices, and since they had no obvious interest in telling anything other than the truth, many people eagerly logged on to their websites. The most famous of these Iraqi 'bloggers', as they were called, called himself 'Salam Pax'. Here he describes a typical night of coalition bombing and Iraqi TV.

The all-clear siren just went on. The bombing would come and go in waves, nothing too heavy and not yet comparable to what was going on in '91. All radio and TV stations are still on, and while the air raid began, the Iraqi TV was showing patriotic songs and didn't even bother to inform viewers that we were under attack. At the moment they are re-airing yesterday's interview with the Minister of Interior Affairs. The sounds of the anti-aircraft **artillery** is still louder than the booms and bangs, which means that they are still far from where we live, but the images we saw on al-Arabia news channel showed a building burning near my aunt's house. We have two safe rooms, one with 'international media' and the other with Iraqi TV on. Everybody is waiting, waiting, waiting. Phones are still OK, we called around the city a moment ago to check on friends. Information is what they need. Iraqi TV says nothing, shows nothing. What good are patriotic songs when bombs are dropping?

Foreign journalists run for cover as a coalition plane flies above the road connecting Baghdad airport with the city centre.

Iraq's neighbours

The countries neighbouring Iraq are all **Muslim** countries, and most of their governments were unwilling to openly support the **coalition's** war against Saddam Hussein. There were two basic reasons for their reluctance. First, they feared that Iraq without Saddam might either break up or turn to Muslim **fundamentalism**, either of which could destabilize the whole region. Secondly, these governments were aware of the anti-American feeling among their own peoples, much of which was caused by US support for Israel in the **Arab-Israeli dispute**.

Two small **Arab** states did support the war: Kuwait provided a base for the coalition armies, and Qatar a base for the coalition headquarters. But the governments of larger Arab states like Egypt, Saudi Arabia and Jordan refused to do so, despite their dependence on American aid and their private desire to see Saddam gone. Turkey, though a fellow member of **NATO**, also refused. Its government feared that Iraq would disintegrate, that the Iraqi **Kurds** would form their own independent state, and that this would encourage Turkey's Kurdish population to demand the same.

Two other neighbours had a further reason to fear the end of Saddam. Iran had been one of the states President Bush included in his 'Axis of Evil', and Syria had frequently been accused by the USA of supporting **terrorism**. Neither of these governments had any love for Saddam, but both feared that their turn might come next.

Muslims in neighbouring Jordan demonstrate against the bombing of Iraq, 21 March 2003.

A Turkish viewpoint

Turkish attitudes to the war were complex. While the Turkish government worried that a war might complicate relations with the Kurds, most Turkish people disliked the idea of a **Western** country attacking a fellow-Muslim country. Turkish student Ozgur Yazici was preparing for his exams when the war began. Here he explains how he and his friends in Trabzon reacted to the events, and how the war has affected the way he sees things.

During the war people here forgot about their economic problems and I forgot about my college exams. People in my country, especially youngsters, felt so hopeless because the only thing we could do was organize anti-war demonstrations and set tables on the street to collect anti-war signatures from people.

Although I knew we would not change anything, we were trying to show that we could come together and make a noise. That was the first time my friends and I had taken to the streets of Trabzon.

The war wasn't necessary. It was successful for the Americans and they have the oil reserves now. I hope the Americans learnt a lesson from all this and I hope they do not think everything will be just fine now. It won't, because the people of Iraq and the whole world saw what happened. People have lots of hatred inside them now – which is not helpful for the future of the world.

Those experiences I had during the war added so much to my life. I feel more mature now and I am more interested in what is happening around me.'

Advance to Baghdad

By the weekend of 29–30 March the sandstorms had cleared, the US forward units (units leading the attack) had been re-supplied, and Iraqi attacks in the towns along the Euphrates had been defeated. The American advance resumed, and by 3 April their forces were within 48 kilometres (30 miles) of Baghdad.

This ground advance was accompanied by a relentless bombing campaign against Iraqi communications and forces. It is unclear what orders were issued to Saddam's **elite** force, the 60,000 strong Iraqi Republican Guard, but whatever they were, they proved ineffective. Many Iraqi officers and men, realizing that the war was lost, deserted and headed for home. Those who tried to fight were destroyed by the **coalition** air forces. The roads to Baghdad were open.

Iraqis leaving the southern city of Basra are searched for weapons by British troops, April 2003.

On 3 April a huge bombing raid cut off the capital's electricity supply, and on the next day US forces seized the city's international airport. Baghdad was now virtually encircled, and US tank units mounted a first raid into the city itself. On 6 April, away to the south, British forces finally moved into central Basra.

The coalition forces were still nervous about sending large forces into the cities, where they might face **sniping**, **suicide bombing** and other forms of enemy activity which were difficult to counter. So, while the bombing continued, small units tested the level of Iraqi resistance by launching raids into the city. On 8 April US Marines set up a base in one of Saddam's abandoned palaces, but there was still no sign of an imminent enemy collapse.

US Marines relax in one Saddam's palaces by the River Tigris, 14 April 2003.

One soldier's war

Interviewed by the BBC, American Staff Sergeant David Richard described his experience of the war.

We left Kuwait on the morning of 19 March and we drove and drove and drove until we got to al-Najaf. I got my first experience of war there. What was it like? Well, it was very tiring, then you get a large adrenaline rush and you fight, and then you feel tired again. It was a real battle and they put up better resistance than we'd expected. Then we rolled up through the outskirts of Karbala and crossed the Euphrates and took up a blocking position. We had to finish off the second armoured brigade of the Medina division of the Republican Guard, though most of it was taken care of by air.

On 5 April my unit did the first run into Baghdad. It was heavily guarded and we were attacked by a suicide bomb vehicle and rocket-propelled grenades and we had to fight all the way in. After that we moved towards the position we're holding now, at the museum. And we took a lot of fire on the way, I can tell you.

Right now I am looking forward to going back to my family who I haven't seen for seven months. How will I feel if there is another war? Well, I am a professional soldier and I'll go where I'm told to go.

The regime collapses

On the morning of 9 April it became clear that the **regime** – its spokesmen, administrators, officials – had disappeared. Realizing that the war was lost, they had taken flight from both the **coalition** forces and their own people. Crowds appeared in the streets, and statues of Saddam were gleefully torn down in front of the TV cameras.

US Marines help locals pull down the huge statue of Saddam in Baghdad. This act came to symbolize the fall of Saddam's dictatorship.

It was far from clear how Iraqis felt about the defeat of Saddam. There were some obvious celebrations, but there were also outbreaks of continuing resistance. Many Iraqis feared that Saddam might still return, and were unwilling to risk showing any pleasure at his removal.

In both Baghdad and Basra most police officers disappeared along with the regime which they had served. It soon became apparent that the US and British governments had made no plans for replacing them, and the coalition military forces lacked both the numbers and the training to fill the gap. As a result, **looting** quickly became widespread. Shops and offices were emptied of everything, hospitals were stripped of life-saving drugs and equipment, and museums were raided of many priceless treasures. The guns discarded by Iraq's beaten army were gathered up by ordinary people for defending their families and property or used by criminals for looting and crime.

The coalition's lack of planning for the post-war phase was also evident in other ways, and the occupation forces were soon being criticized for their inability to restore electricity or running water. The difficulties of restoring Iraq to normality – let alone transforming it into a working **democracy** – were already becoming apparent.

Days of looting
In the days which followed the end of large-scale fighting, the **Western media** featured many eyewitness reports of widespread looting. Such reports, like this one published in the *Guardian* newspaper, emphasized the coalition's failure to restore law and order.

The Guardian

April 2003

Using wheelbarrows and donkey carts, pickup trucks and their own elbow grease, [hard physical labour] Iraqis rolled their parade of war booty through the streets. Smoke from dozens of fires hung over Baghdad as the city gave itself over to the looting, which spread from government warehouses and buildings to hotels and private shops. By afternoon, the central bank and several ministries had been attacked. The mob had also arrived at the social security directorate and the television head-quarters and plundered at least two **UN** offices.

A spokeswoman for the International Red Cross said that the al-Kindi hospital near the centre of Baghdad was attacked by armed looters who stripped it of everything, including beds, electrical fittings and medical equipment. Elsewhere looters drove tractors, pick-up trucks and trailers, and even a large bus, up to a villa belonging to Tariq Aziz, Saddam's deputy prime minister, stealing everything from paintings to curtains, and even stripping the electrical wires from the main switchboard. His library was ransacked, although the looters did leave behind a book on geopolitics by Richard Nixon, the 'Godfather' novels of Mario Puzo, and the complete works of Saddam in Arabic.

Short-term priorities

By 14 April the northern cities of Kirkuk, Mosul and Tikrit had also fallen to the advancing US forces. **Kurdish** fighters played a prominent role in taking the first two, which prompted loud protests from Turkey. But the Kurdish leaders denied any desire for an independent state. All they wanted, they said, was a degree of self-government in the new Iraq.

Once the large-scale fighting was over, the **coalition** forces began looking for the leaders of the fallen **regime**. The US government issued a list of the 52 'most wanted' leaders. Over the next few months around 40 of these fugitives were killed, captured or gave themselves up. Saddam's two sons, Qusay and Uday, were killed in a gun battle in Mosul on 22 July, but Saddam himself was not captured until December, in a small village just south of Tikrit.

Restoring law and order proved extremely difficult. The disappearance of the old regime's police, the flood of available weaponry, and the fact that Saddam had opened the prisons before the war started, all encouraged lawlessness. The coalition leadership's failure to foresee the problem, and their slowness in dealing with it, made things worse.

Other coalition priorities were the repair of Iraq's **infrastructure**, the delivery of food and medical aid, and the creation of a new Iraqi government. The plan was for the coalition to appoint an **interim administration** which would organize elections, probably in 2005. In the meantime, real power would remain with the occupying powers.

US soldiers distribute food and other supplies to Iraqi citizens living near Nasiriyah.

Planning a future for Iraq

On 15 April 2003 a selection of prominent Iraqis were invited to Nasiriyah by the US government for talks about the future of Iraq. At the end of the talks the following 13-point statement was issued. Reading between the lines it is easy to see what worries were expressed at the meeting. Point 5, for example, was presumably insisted on by those **secular** Iraqis who oppose a narrow **Islamic** view of the role of women.

13-point statement on a democratic Iraq

1. Iraq must be **democratic**.

2. A future government should not be based on communal identity [identification with a particular **ethnic** group].

3. A future government should be organized as a democratic federal system [a system in which a country's states or provinces have powers to run their own affairs].

4. The rule of law must be paramount [supreme].

5. Iraq must be built on a respect for diversity, including respect for the role of women.

6. The meeting discussed the role of religion in state and society.

7. The meeting discussed the principle that Iraqis must choose their leaders, not have them imposed from outside.

8. That political violence must be rejected and reconstruction begun.

9. That Iraqis and the coalition must work together to restore security and basic services.

10. That the **Ba'ath** Party must be dissolved.

11. That there should be an open dialogue with all national groups.

12. That the meeting condemned **looting** and the destruction of documents.

13. That the meeting voted to hold another meeting in ten days.

New international tensions

The run-up to the war had left a lingering mistrust between governments which normally considered themselves **allies**. The British and US governments felt they had been let down by the governments of France, Germany, Russia and other countries. These governments, they claimed, were unwilling to offer support when it mattered.

For their part, the French and their allies resented the **coalition** partners' disregard of majority opinion, and complained of the damage their unauthorized action had done to **UN** authority. One way of healing the rift would have been to let the UN supervise the rebuilding of post-war Iraq, but the coalition partners were unwilling. They had fought the war, they said, and they would supervise the peace.

The arguments were presented as political arguments, but all the governments concerned were also influenced by money. The USA and the UK believed they could make a lot of money from Iraqi oil and the rebuilding of Iraq. The French and Russians had signed big oil production contracts with Saddam's **regime**, and wanted to see them honoured by any new Iraqi government. The USA and the UK, however, were in physical possession of the country. The war had only been over a few days when the first large rebuilding contract was handed out. It went to the US Halliburton Corporation, which included Vice-President Dick Cheney among its former chief executives. In the months that followed, companies from countries which had opposed the war were refused permission to bid for similar reconstruction contracts.

Iraqi children sit in the ruins of a military compound destroyed during the war. They are trying to make a living by recycling bricks and metals from the rubble.

Iraqi oil

Iraq's crucial importance as a future source of oil was recognized by both supporters and opponents of the war. In this lead editorial, published soon after the fighting ended, the *New York Times* argued that the victorious coalition partners would be condemned by world opinion if they attempted to secure Iraq's oil wealth purely for their own benefit.

The New York Times

April 2003

Iraq is no longer a republic of fear, but it is still a republic of oil. Some 112 billion barrels lie beneath its soil, more than a tenth of the world's known reserves. How the Bush administration handles the management of that resource as it gains control of the country will go a long way toward determining not just the future of Iraq but also America's worldwide reputation. Any effort to manipulate Iraq's oil for the benefit of the United States and American oil companies rather than the benefit of the Iraqi people will squander whatever political gains Washington has won in the war.

A country rich in oil: a worker checking oil production at the North Oil Company in Kirkuk, northern Iraq in April 2003.

New tensions inside Iraq

In the aftermath of the war there were considerable tensions inside Iraq. For one thing, the relationship between the **coalition** occupying forces and the local population was far from easy. For another, the different **ethnic**, religious and political groups inside Iraq that had clashed in the past, were now able to express any disagreements they might have on the direction their country should take.

An Iraqi girl shows support for the US occupation. Her family are waiting to find out if a relative is in a nearby prisoner-of-war camp.

There was a widespread hope, particularly in the USA, that the coalition's forces would be welcomed as 'liberators' by the majority of Iraqi people. This did not prove to be the case. Many were grateful for Saddam's removal, but there was also resentment towards the invaders. When the coalition forces proved incapable of swiftly restoring order and a working **infrastructure**, the gratitude began to fade and the resentment to grow. Resistance to the occupation continued. Attacks on coalition forces happened every day, and the number of Americans killed after the war soon outnumbered those killed during the war itself. Hundreds of Iraqis were also killed in frequent **terrorist** bombings. At first, the coalition claimed that the resistance was being mounted by remnants of Saddam's **regime**, but as the months went by it became clear that anti-Saddam Iraqis and **Islamic** fighters from outside the country were equally involved in the anti-occupation demonstrations and attacks.

In these same months, there were signs of the potential for conflict between Iraq's ethnic, religious and political groups. There were serious incidents of violence between **Kurds** and Arabs, and calls from some **Shi'a** religious leaders for an **Islamic republic**. These calls have alarmed those Iraqis who prefer life in an essentially **secular** state. Over the next few years Iraq's ethnic and religious communities will have to reach agreement on some very divisive issues.

The Guardian

3 May 2003

Sheikh Mohammed al-Yacobi told the *Guardian*: 'Ninety-eight per cent of the people are **Muslims**. The Iraqi constitution must not commit to anything that will go against **Islamic** law.'

Sheikh Mohammed al-Tabatabi told worshippers: 'The **West** calls for freedom and liberty. Islam is not calling for this... True liberty is obedience to God and to be liberated from desires. The danger we should anticipate in the coming days is the danger to our religion from the West trying to spread pornographic magazines and TV channels.'

Under Saddam, Iraq was a secular society. Women had equal rights with men and freedom to dress in Western clothes. It was more lax than many of its neighbours about alcohol. But Sheikh Tabatabi said: 'We would not allow shops to sell alcohol.' He added that women should not be allowed to walk around unveiled.

A third cleric, Quais al-Khazaalym, said: 'I think the right decision is to have an Islamic state. If the US blocks such a state and people want it, this will lead to lots of trouble with the US.'

Iraqi Shi'a Muslims protest against the arrest of one of their religious leaders, a prominent opponent of the US-appointed Iraqi governing council.

47

Prospects

Early in 2004 the Bush administration announced that it would hand power to the Iraqi Governing Council in June of that year, but also made it clear that **coalition** troops would remain in the country for several years. Many Iraqis distrusted the American-appointed Governing Council, and continued to demand elections before any transfer of power. In the meantime, much of the country's **infrastructure** remained in ruins, and the violence continued.

The old Iraq has been pulled down, but it is too soon to judge how much of an improvement the new Iraq will be. It is possible that the hopes of those who supported the war will be realized, and that Iraq will be slowly transformed into a modern, prosperous **democracy**. It is also possible that relations inside Iraq – both between Iraqis and with the foreign occupation forces – will dramatically worsen, encouraging extremism and violence, and threatening the country's unity. Although

a major source of **terrorism** has been destroyed, the conditions for another may have been created. Much depends on how the occupiers behave, and on whose interests they put first – the Iraqis' or their own.

Members of the new Governing Council, on stage at a Baghdad convention centre, July 2003.

Iraq's success or failure over the coming months and years will profoundly affect the rest of the world. The difficulties of the first few months have re-raised questions about the wisdom of the war, and the failure to find **weapons of mass destruction** has raised doubts about the honesty of the arguments used to justify it. But if the policy of the US **neo-conservatives** – of aggressively pursuing any state which poses a possible threat to the USA or its **allies** – does prove a lasting success in Iraq, then other states can expect to receive similar visitations. It remains to be seen whether this will make the world a safer or a more dangerous place.

Just a beginning

Lawrence Kaplan and William Cristol are influential US journalists, and supporters of a 'neo-conservative' US foreign policy (Cristol was one of those who signed the letter to President Clinton quoted on page 17). Here, in a passage from their book *The War Over Iraq*, which was written shortly before the war was fought, they argue that the overthrow of Saddam's **regime** would be only the first of many such steps needed to secure a US-friendly world.

A strong America, capable of projecting force quickly and with devastating effect to important regions of the world, would make it less likely that other states would try to alter the status quo [existing situation] in their favour. The message we should be sending to potential enemies is: 'Don't even think about it'…

The mission begins in Baghdad, but it does not end there. Were the United States to retreat after victory into complacency and self-absorption, as it did the last time it went to war in Iraq, new dangers would soon arise. Preventing this outcome will be a burden, of which the war in Iraq represents but the first instalment. But America cannot escape its responsibility for maintaining a decent world order. The answer to this challenge is the American idea itself [of individual rights and freedoms], and behind it the unparalleled military and economic strength of the country. Duly armed, the United States can act to secure its safety and to advance the cause of liberty – in Baghdad and beyond.

Burning oil from a ruptured pipeline spews black smoke into the Iraqi sky in August 2003. Pipelines became an increasingly popular target for supporters of Saddam Hussein and others who were determined to resist the US occupation.

What have we learnt from the war in Iraq?

Two lessons seem clear from the months leading up to the war. First, the **United Nations** was shown to be powerless when one or more leading states refuse to abide by the wishes of the majority. Secondly, in most of those countries whose governments supported the war, a majority of people were clearly opposed to it, but their opposition made no difference to the eventual decision. This, and the later revelations of deceit by those same governments – such as the discrediting of the earlier British government claim that Saddam could fire off **weapons of mass destruction** at 45 minutes' notice – are bound to have undermined faith in **democracy**.

The war itself confirmed that control of the sky is always a recipe for military success. It also offered proof that modern weaponry can now limit civilian casualties to an extent almost unimaginable only ten years ago. However, something as simple as a sandstorm can still upset the most sophisticated army.

The basic lesson of the post-war months was that an extended occupation is always resented, no matter how well-meaning the motivation behind it. The US and British governments have placed themselves in a difficult and dangerous situation, one that they can neither abandon nor easily sort out.

Overall, the war offered stark confirmation of US power. The USA now dominates world affairs as no other single state has done for centuries. It can win any war it wishes to fight. Whether it can translate such victories into a peace that others find acceptable will be the most crucial political question of the early 21st century.

An Iraqi's view of the war

Mukhallad al-Sinwai is a 36-year-old Iraqi pharmacist. Here he talks about his experience of the war, and how he thinks it has changed his country.

The fighting in Nasiriyah went on for many days. It came close to us. **Artillery** fire fell two metres from our house and everything broke – the windows, the glasses, and the house shook like an earthquake. There was also a lot of random shooting, which is how the old woman next door was killed, by bullets coming in through the window.

I did not agree with the reasons for the war. I don't believe Bush's excuse that we had illegal weapons. But I am happy to see the end of Saddam Hussein. I am a **Shi'a Muslim,** and he did terrible things to the Shi'as.

But while the Americans and British talk about a 'free Iraq' it does not feel free. It will not be free until their armies have gone. Now at least we can talk about things openly. Before, if we talked about the **regime,** it had to be in whispers. Walls have ears, is what we used to say. So, it is a liberation.

Poor Iraqi families living in a ruined section of Baghdad, September 2003. It is often women and young children who suffer most once war is over as medical supplies and health care services are disrupted.

51

Timeline

1918		Britain takes control of Iraq from defeated Turks
1932		Britain recognizes Iraq's independence
1958	July	Iraqi military officers overthrow the British-supported monarchy
1968	July	**Ba'ath** Party seizes power in Iraq
1968–72		Saddam Hussein gradually assumes dictatorial powers
1972		Nationalization of the Iraqi Petroleum Company
1980–8		Iraq-Iran war
1988	March	**Chemical weapons** used against **Kurds** in Halabja
1990	August	Iraq invades Kuwait
1991	Jan–Feb	Iraq ejected from Kuwait
1991–98		**UN** weapon inspectors in Iraq
2001	11 September	**Terrorist** attacks on World Trade Center, New York and Pentagon, Washington
	Oct–Nov	US-led **coalition** attacks Afghanistan as part of a new 'War on Terrorism'
2002	January	George W. Bush gives 'Axis of Evil' speech
	September	Iraq invites weapon inspectors to return
	November	**UN resolution** 1441 sets conditions for return of weapons inspectors
2003	February	USA and Britain call for second UN resolution to trigger war. Opposition from **Security Council** members France, Russia and Germany, and many other countries.
	Feb–Mar	Mass protests around the world against a war
	March	Dates in brackets: (17) USA delivers ultimatum to Saddam; Robin Cook resigns from British Government; (19) Bombing of Baghdad begins overnight; (20) First US/UK forces move into Iraq, southern oilfields secured: (21) UK forces take al-Faw Peninsula, US forces reach Nasiriyah; (23) US forces halted at Nasiriyah and Najaf; (25) Fierce sandstorms hinder military operations; (26) Civilians killed in Baghdad market bombing, battle for Najaf; (26–29) Pause in advance; (31) US forces 32 kilometres (50 miles) from Baghdad
	April	(1–2) US advances; (3) Bombing cuts power in Baghdad; (4) US takes Baghdad Airport; (5) US tanks into outskirts of Baghdad; (6) UK tanks into central Basra, US tanks raid Baghdad city centre; (9) US marines take city, **regime** melts away, Saddam statues destroyed; (10) **Looting** begins in Baghdad, Kurds take Kirkuk; (11) US/Kurds take Mosul, Baghdad descends into anarchy; (14) US forces seize Saddam's hometown Tikrit
	Apr–Dec	Continuing problems restoring rule of law and power supply. Continuing violent resistance to occupation. First steps taken towards creating a new Iraqi government. Continuing arguments about whether the war was legal, necessary or wise.
	July 22	Saddam's sons Uday and Qusay are killed in Mosul
	October	World governments pledge $37.5 billion in aid and loans for the reconstruction of Iraq
	Nov 15	US announces that coalition will hand over power to Iraqi Governing Council in July 2004
	Dec 13	Saddam Hussein captured just outside Tikrit
2004	Jan 28	David Kay, head of the US weapons inspector in Iraq, tells US **Congress** that Saddam Hussein almost certainly had no **weapons of mass destruction** before the previous year's war
	Jan–March	Violent attacks on coalition forces and Iraqi civilian targets continue
	March 8	US-appointed Governing Council signs interim constitution

Find out more

Books & websites

The Gulf War, Dr John King (Wayland, 1994)
Saddam Hussein and Iraq, David Downing (Heinemann Library, 2002)

http://www.heinemannexplore.co.uk
Go Exploring! Log on to Heinemann's online history resource.

http://www.guardian.co.uk/Archive/0,4271,,00.html
This site has newspaper articles on recent and current events in Iraq.

http://news.bbc.co.uk/1/hi/in_depth/middle_east/2002/conflict_with_iraq
Website containing information on the causes, course and aftermath of the war.

http://www.cnn.com/World
CNN world news website.

List of primary sources

The author and publisher gratefully acknowledge the following publications from which written sources in the book are drawn. In some cases the wording or sentence structure has been simplified to make the material more appropriate for a school readership.

p9.   *The Times,* 24.7.58
p11.   *Republic of Fear,* Kanan Makiya, (University of California Press, 1998)
p13.   Senate Foreign Relations Report, cited by Mical L. Sifry and Christopher Cerf (eds), *The Iraq War Reader* (Touchstone, 2003)
p15.   The *Guardian,* 19.9.2002
p17.   Letter to President Clinton, cited by Mical L. Sifry and Christopher Cerf (eds.), *The Iraq War Reader* (Touchstone, 2003)
p19.   George W. Bush's State of the Union address, cited by Mical L. Sifry and Christopher Cerf (eds.), *The Iraq War Reader* (Touchstone, 2003)
p21.   http://news.bbc.co.uk/1/hi/in_depth/middle_east/2002/conflict_with_iraq/2281452.stm
p23.   http://www.timesonline.co.uk/article/0,,482-543296,00.html
p25.   http://.bbc.co.uk/1/hi/uk_politics/2859431.stm
p27.   http://www.guardian.co.uk/print/0,3858,4601559-103681,00.html
p29.   http://news.bbc.co.uk/1/hi/in_depth/middle_east/2002/conflict_with_iraq/default.stm
p31.   Report by Clive Myrie, cited by Sarah Beck and Malcolm Downing (ed.s), *BBC News: The Battle for Iraq* (BBC, 2003)
p33.   Robert Fisk, in the *Independent,* 27.3.2003
p35.   Report by 'Salam Pax', cited by Randeep Ramesh (ed.), *The War We Could Not Stop* (Faber and Faber, 2003)
p37.   http://news.bbc.co.uk/1/hi/in_depth/middle_east/2002/conflict_with_iraq/default.stm
p39.   http://news.bbc.co.uk/1/hi/in_depth/middle_east/2002/conflict_with_iraq/default.stm
p41.   http://www.guardian.co.uk/international/story/0,3604,934236,00.html
p43.   http://www.guardian.co.uk/international/story/0,3604,937855,00.html
p45.   *New York Times,* 11.4.03
p47.   Ewen MacAskill, in the *Guardian,* 3.5.2003
p49.   Lawrence Kaplan and William Cristol, cited by Mical L. Sifry and Christopher Cerf (eds.), *The Iraq War Reader* (Touchstone, 2003)
p51.   http://news.bbc.co.uk/1/hi/in_depth/middle_east/2002/conflict_with_iraq/default.stm

Glossary

allies persons, groups or states who come together in order to help each other reach a common goal

al-Qaeda Islamic fundamentalist terrorist group which also acts as an umbrella organization, financing and helping to plan terrorist acts by other smaller groups around the world. It has been responsible for – among others – the African embassy attacks of 1998, the 9/11 attacks of 2001 and the Bali bombing of 2002.

Arab member of a people which originated in present-day Arabia, and which now forms by far the largest group in most countries of the Middle East and North Africa. Most but not all Arabs are Arabic-speaking Muslims.

Arab-Israeli dispute dispute between Israel and the Palestinian Arabs over how the former territory of Palestine should be divided

Arab nationalist one who believes in the idea that Arab interests can best be promoted through Arab unity, and perhaps even the creation of a single Arab state

artillery heavy guns used in land warfare, usually mounted on wheels or tracks

authorization official permission

Ba'ath Arab nationalist movement which has formed political parties in several Arab states. Ba'ath parties have ruled Syria since the 1960s and Iraq between 1968 and 2003.

bankrupt having no money, and unable to pay debts

biased seeing something from a prejudiced point of view

biological weapons weapons employing viruses/bacteria found in nature

chemical weapons weapons employing synthetic poisons

coalition alliance of two or more nations, parties or other groups

Cold War name given to the hostility that existed between the free enterprise capitalist and communist worlds between 1947 and the late 1980s

Congress the law-making arm of the US government, comprising the Senate and House of Representatives

containment keeping in, restraining or enclosing

coup violent seizure of power

cruise missiles missiles that can be fired from land, sea or air, and which can have their direction changed while in flight

democracy political system in which governments are regularly elected by the mass of the people, or a country in which this system exists

Democrat supporter or member of the Democratic Party, one of the two major US political parties

dossier collection of facts or documents concerned with a particular subject

economic sanctions policy of refusing to trade with a particular country, either in one particular product or in all products

elite group of people considered to be the best within a larger group, usually in terms of their wealth, power and talent

embedded in the war on Iraq, word used to describe journalists permanently attached to particular units of the armed forces

ethnic relating to different tribal or racial groups

European Union still-expanding organization of European states which was created to remove economic and political barriers between them

free enterprise way of organizing the economy that relies on individuals rather than government making the decisions about which goods and services are produced, and how they are bought and sold

Free Officers groups of nationalistic army officers in both Egypt and Iraq who opposed continuing British influence over their governments

friendly fire fire from one's own side

fundamentalism returning to the basics of any religion or ideology, which often involves supporting what are now considered old-fashioned social and political ideas

Gulf War name usually given to the war fought in early 1991 by a US-led coalition to reverse the previous year's Iraqi invasion of Kuwait. The name has also been applied to the Iran-Iraq War of 1980-88.

infrastructure economic foundations of a society

interim government temporary administration with the job of setting up a permanent government

Islam one of the world's major three monotheistic (one God) religions (along with Christianity and Judaism), founded by the Prophet Mohammed in the 7th century

Islamic republic government which bases its laws on the laws of Islam

Kurds people who live in Kurdistan, a region of the Middle East which includes large parts of Turkey, Iraq and Iran. Most Kurds are Sunni Muslims.

looting stealing from shops and other businesses, usually when law and order has temporarily broken down

media means of mass communication, like TV, radio, newspapers, etc

mortar portable cannon for firing explosive shells

Muslim follower of Islam

NATO North Atlantic Treaty Organization – an alliance of European and North American states which was formed in 1948 to oppose the Soviet Union

neo-conservative literally, new or modern conservative. In the US the term has been used to describe politicians who believe that America should aggressively make the most of its position as the world's only superpower.

no-fly zone area in which it is forbidden to fly. The Iraqi Air Force was forbidden to fly in two such zones by the USA and Britain between 1991 and 2003.

nuclear weapons bombs or missiles which rely on the release of energy through combining or separating atoms

Ottoman Empire empire established by the Ottoman tribe of Turks in the thirteenth century which at its height included most of the Middle East and much of south-east Europe. The empire finally came to an end in 1918.

pre-emptive attacking first to defeat an expected attack

primary source direct evidence about historical events

propaganda promotion of ideas, often involving a selective version of the truth

regime government

Republican in the USA, supporter or member of the Republican Party

saboteur someone who takes action to try to hinder or prevent the achievement of an aim

secondary source historical account written some time after the events described have taken place

secular unconcerned with religion or religious identities

Security Council council within the United Nations most responsible for the maintenance of world peace and security.

It has five permanent members – the USA, Russia, Britain, France and China – and ten rotating members chosen from other member states.

security police police concerned with the security of the regime in power

Shi'a Muslims smaller of two major Muslim groups, which originated in a dispute over who should lead all Muslims

sniping in war, firing shots from hiding, usually at long range

sorties operational military flights

State of the Union address speech given to Congress each year by the president of the USA

suicide bomber person who deliberately blows himself or herself up in order to kill others

Sunni Muslims larger of two major Muslim groups, which originated in a dispute over who should lead all Muslims

superpower most powerful nation or nations. The USA has been considered the only superpower since the break-up of the Soviet Union in 1991.

terrorism use of violence against civilians to achieve political ends

totalitarian demanding obedience from all citizens in all areas of life

United Nations (UN) international organization set up in 1945 to help settle disputes between nations and increase international cooperation

United Nations resolution new ruling or law put forward for voting on

veto a no-vote. In the United Nations Security Council a single veto from any of the five permanent members – the US, Britain, China, France and Russia – is enough to defeat any proposal.

War on Terrorism worldwide campaign to eliminate terrorism which began in September 2001

weapons of mass destruction weapons capable of killing thousands, or laying waste large areas, at single blow. They are usually sub-divided into nuclear, chemical and biological weapons.

West (Western) when used with a capital 'w', usually refers to Europe and those parts of the world – most notably, North America and Australasia – permanently settled by Europeans.

Index

Titles in the *Witness to History* series include:

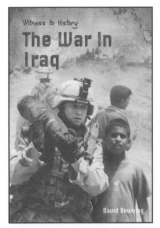

Hardback   0 431 17074-6

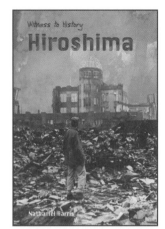

Hardback   0 431 17055-X

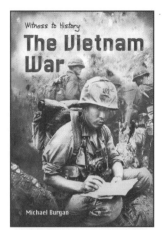

Hardback   0 431 17054-1

Hardback   0 431 17057-6

Hardback   0 431 17056-8

Hardback   0 431 17064-9

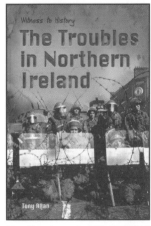

Hardback   0 431 17067-3

Hardback   0 431 17066-5

Find out about the other titles in this series on our website www.heinemann.co.uk/library